CHANITA R. RAMSEY

As the Deer Pants After the Water

Devotional Companion Study Guide

First edition

ISBN: 978-1-970671-09-4

This book was professionally typeset on Reedsy. Find out more at reedsy.com

Contents

Introduction

Welcome to the As the Deer Pants After the Water Devotional Companion Study Guide. If you're holding this in your hands, it's not by accident. Something in your heart is crying out for more—for peace, for healing, for clarity, for love that lasts. This guide was created just for you—a woman who has been wounded by toxic love, who has wrestled with loneliness, and who is now ready to walk in wholeness and divine intimacy.

This isn't just a workbook. It's a sacred space for you to exhale. A space to process what you've read in the book, but more than that—a space to meet God in your most honest places.

You'll find:

- Weekly Devotional Reflections that echo the heart of each chapter
- Anchor Scriptures to remind you of God's truth
- Reflection Questions and Journal Prompts to help you process what's in your heart
- Prayers to guide your conversations with God
- Action Steps to help you apply what you're learning
- And God's Whisper—a gentle love letter from your Heavenly Father, written just for you.

Whether you're doing this study alone, with a small group, or journaling in quiet moments, I want you to know this: you are not alone. God sees every step you've taken to survive—and now, He wants to teach you how to thrive.

Take your time. Don't rush the healing process. Some days will feel heavy, others freeing. But in it all, God will be right here with you—leading, loving, and reminding you that you are His.

Drink deeply, daughter. The living water your soul has been longing for is already flowing.

With love and hope,

Chanita R. Ramsey

Author & Sister in the Journey

How to Use This Guide

This devotional study guide is designed to help you engage your heart, spirit, and mind as you reflect on the truths in As the Deer Pants After the Water book. Each section is a tool—not a task—to help you move from brokenness into wholeness, from toxic love into God's love.

Here's how each chapter is laid out:

1. Chapter Theme Recap

A short reflection that highlights the key message from the chapter.

2. Anchor Scripture

A foundational verse to meditate on and carry with you.

3. Devotional Thought

A fresh insight or expansion of the chapter's message to stir your heart.

4. Reflection Questions

These questions help you examine your emotions, behaviors, and beliefs in light of God's truth. Be honest—this is your safe place.

5. Journal Prompt

Use this prompt to write freely. Let the Holy Spirit guide your pen. There are no rules here.

6. Prayer

Each prayer is a starting point. Let it lead you into your own personal conversation with God.

7. Action Step

One practical thing you can do this week to begin living out what you're learning.

8. God's Whisper

A short, intimate letter written as if God is speaking directly to you. Read it slowly. Let it settle deep into your soul.

A Few Suggestions:

- Go at your own pace. This is not a race. If one week takes you two or even three—so be it. Healing takes time.
- Be honest. God can handle your truth. This is a safe space to be real.
- Use a journal. If space runs out, grab a notebook to keep all your thoughts in one sacred place.
- Pray first. Before each session, invite the Holy Spirit to meet you right

where you are.

Most of all, know this: God is not in a hurry with you. He's simply asking you to draw near and drink deeply.

Prayer for the Journey

Dear Heavenly Father,

I come before You with an open heart and a soul that's thirsty for healing. I've been through things I'm still trying to understand, and I carry wounds I don't always know how to speak about. But I believe You are the God who sees, the One who heals, and the only love that truly satisfies.

As I begin this devotional journey, I invite You into every broken place within me.

Into the memories that still sting.

Into the moments I've tried to forget.

Into the patterns I've repeated out of pain.

I invite You into it all.

Give me the courage to be honest, even when it hurts.

Give me the strength to let go, even when it's hard.

And give me the grace to receive Your love, even when I feel unworthy.

I surrender this process to You.

I'm not here to impress You—I'm here to be transformed by You.

Do what only You can do in my life.

May every page of this guide be a step toward freedom.

May every tear water the seeds of something new.

And may I leave this journey stronger, wiser, and more in love with You than ever before.

In Jesus' name,

Amen.

Week 1: What Are You Really Thirsty For?

Theme Recap

We all long for something. Love. Security. Belonging. But too often, we run to people, pleasures, or patterns that promise to quench that thirst—only to leave us emptier than before. This week invites you to take an honest look at what you've been running to, and begin turning your heart toward the only One who truly satisfies.

Anchor Scripture

"As the deer pants for the water brooks, so pants my soul for You, O God."
  —Psalm 42:1 (NKJV)

Devotional Thought

Have you ever been so thirsty that water felt like salvation in a glass? That's the kind of thirst our souls experience when we've been giving our love to people who can't love us back. You may have chased someone's attention or approval, hoping it would finally make you feel worthy. But the truth is, anything outside of God will eventually leave you parched.

God is not mad at your thirst—He created it. He just wants to fill it with Himself.

He is the Living Water. The Well that never runs dry.

He doesn't offer temporary affection. He offers eternal love.
This week is about pausing long enough to recognize the difference.

Reflection Questions

1. What have you been thirsting for most in this season of your life?
2. Who or what have you turned to in the past to satisfy that longing?
3. How has that left you feeling in the long run—closer to God or farther from Him?
4. What would it look like to turn that same desire toward God?

Journal Prompt

Write a letter to God today, honestly telling Him what you've been chasing and why. Be real with your pain. Let the tears fall if they must. End your letter by asking Him to help you thirst for Him more than anything or anyone else.

Prayer

Lord, I admit that I've been running to broken wells, expecting them to fill a deep need in me. I've looked for love in places that only left me more empty. But I'm here now, ready to drink from You. Help me thirst for Your presence, Your peace, and Your truth above everything else. Teach me how to let go of what doesn't satisfy, and fill me with living water that never runs dry. In Jesus' name, amen.

Action Step

This week, commit to starting each day with 10 minutes of quiet time with God—no phone, no distractions. Read Psalm 42 slowly. Ask God to awaken your spiritual thirst for Him in a new way.

God's Whisper

My daughter, I see the longing in your soul. I know the ache behind your choices. But I'm not here to condemn you—I'm here to fill you. You don't have to earn My love or chase it down. It's already yours. Come to Me, again and again. I will never run dry.

Week 1: What Are You Really Thirsty For?

Day 1: Recognize Your Thirst

Scripture: Psalm 42:1
   "As the deer pants for the water brooks, so pants my soul for You, O God."
   Instruction: Today, begin by simply acknowledging the deep thirst in your soul. What have you been craving or chasing that hasn't truly satisfied? Take a moment to sit quietly and listen to what your heart says.
   Reflection: In your journal, write down what you feel most thirsty for—love, acceptance, peace, security, or something else.
   Action: Set aside 5 minutes of quiet time today to meditate on Psalm 42:1. Visualize yourself as the deer, desperately seeking water. Ask God to help you see what you're really thirsting for.

Day 2: Identify Your Broken Wells

Scripture: Jeremiah 2:13
   "My people have committed two sins: They have forsaken me, the spring of living water, and have dug their own cisterns, broken cisterns that cannot hold water."
   Instruction: Reflect on the "broken wells" in your life—people, habits, or things you've relied on to fill your soul but never truly satisfied.
   Reflection: Write in your journal about where you've been digging for

satisfaction outside of God. How have these things left you feeling empty?

Action: Ask God to reveal any false sources of hope or love in your life. Pray for the strength to turn away from them.

Day 3: Longing for True Living Water

Scripture: John 4:13-14

"Everyone who drinks this water will be thirsty again, but whoever drinks the water I give them will never thirst."

Instruction: Jesus promises living water that quenches forever. Today, focus on God's invitation to drink deeply from Him.

Reflection: Journal your thoughts on what it would mean to thirst after God alone. How does this challenge or encourage you?

Action: Find a quiet place and spend 10 minutes in prayer, asking God to satisfy your deepest longings with His presence.

Day 4: Turning Your Heart Toward God

Scripture: Psalm 63:1

"O God, you are my God; earnestly I seek you; my soul thirsts for you; my flesh faints for you."

Instruction: Today, choose to turn your heart fully toward God, consciously deciding to seek Him before anything else.

Reflection: Write a prayer or letter to God expressing your desire to know Him more deeply and to be filled by Him.

Action: Practice a simple breathing prayer today—inhale slowly, saying "Jesus," exhale, saying "fill me." Repeat for 5 minutes.

Day 5: Letting Go of the Old

Scripture: Isaiah 43:18-19

"Forget the former things; do not dwell on the past. See, I am doing a new thing!"

Instruction: Recognize that holding on to past hurts or false hopes keeps you thirsty. God wants to do a new thing in you.

Reflection: Journal about one thing you need to release to God this week—a relationship, a habit, or a belief.

Action: Write that "thing" on a piece of paper and symbolically give it to God through prayer or burning (safely).

Day 6: Receiving God's Living Water

Scripture: Revelation 22:17

"Let the one who is thirsty come; let the one who wishes take the free gift of the water of life."

Instruction: God freely offers living water—His love and grace are never earned, only received.

Reflection: Write about how it feels to know God offers you His love freely. What fears or doubts come up? How can you trust Him more?

Action: Spend time resting in God's presence today. You might sit quietly, listen to worship music, or read a Psalm aloud.

Day 7: Drinking Deeply and Walking Forward

Scripture: Psalm 36:8

"They feast on the abundance of your house; you give them drink from your river of delights."

Instruction: Celebrate the progress you've made this week. Drinking deeply from God's river of delights is not a one-time event but a lifelong journey.

Reflection: Write a letter to your future self encouraging her to keep seeking God's living water.

Action: Plan a weekly time for quiet reflection or prayer moving forward, committing to nurture your soul's thirst for God.

Week 1 Group Discussion Questions: What Are You Really Thirsty For?

1. Opening: What stood out to you most from this week's devotional? Was there a moment that felt especially personal or challenging?
2. Psalm 42:1 compares our soul's thirst to a deer panting for water. How would you describe your own spiritual thirst right now? What do you feel your soul is craving most?
3. What are some "broken wells" or false sources of satisfaction you've chased in the past? How did they leave you feeling?
4. Why do you think it's so easy to try to fill our deepest needs with people or things instead of God?
5. The devotional invites us to turn our hearts fully toward God's living water. What are some practical ways you can do that in your daily life?
6. What fears or doubts come up when you consider trusting God to satisfy your deepest needs?
7. How can this group support each other in choosing to thirst after God rather than temporary things?

Closing Prayer:

Lord, thank You for seeing me and not turning away. Thank You for being a safe place where I can bring my longings, my shame, and my hunger. I want more of You. Teach me to come to You first, and to trust that You will satisfy every need. Amen.

Healing Activity: "The Deep Well" Visualization

Instructions:

Find a quiet space. Close your eyes and imagine a deep well in front of you. See Jesus standing beside it, offering you living water. In your mind, imagine yourself handing Him your thirst—every unmet need, every broken craving, every false source. Picture Him filling you instead with joy, peace, and belonging. Sit in this moment and let Him speak to your heart.

Afterward, write down anything He said to you or what you felt during the visualization.

Week 2: Letting Go and Learning to Trust God's Love

Theme Recap:

This week is all about surrender. Letting go of toxic attachments, broken beliefs, and survival mechanisms that kept you bound—but never healed you. It's about learning to trust God's love over what's familiar. His love doesn't manipulate, disappoint, or abandon. It restores, redeems, and invites you into rest.

Anchor Scripture:

"Trust in the Lord with all your heart and lean not on your own understanding; in all your ways submit to Him, and He will make your paths straight."
  – Proverbs 3:5–6 (NIV)

Devotional Thought:

Sometimes the hardest thing to let go of is the version of love we thought we needed. We hold on because it feels safer than the unknown. But God's love is not a gamble—it's a guarantee. His love will never exploit you or make you prove your worth. As you release what was never meant to stay, you'll begin to see that you were never empty—you were just giving too much of yourself to what couldn't fill you. Trusting God's love starts with a single decision: to believe that He is better.

Reflection Questions:

1. What are you still holding on to that God is asking you to release?
2. What fears come up when you think about letting go?
3. In what ways has your view of love been shaped by pain rather than truth?

Journal Prompt:

Write a list titled: "What I'm afraid to let go of—and why." Then beside each item, write what God's truth says about it. End your journal by writing: "God, I choose to trust You more than I trust my fear."

Prayer:

Father, I've clung to things that made me feel safe, even when they were hurting me. I confess that I've struggled to trust Your love. Today, I give You my grip. I release the people, places, and patterns that no longer serve the woman You're calling me to be. Teach me to trust again. Teach me to trust You. In Jesus' name, amen.

Action Step:

Write down the name of the person, memory, or pattern you're letting go of. Place it in a jar, tear it up, or bury it in the ground. Let this be a physical act of spiritual release.

God's Whisper:

Beloved, I know it's hard to trust when your heart has been mishandled. But I will not break your heart—I will heal it. Let Me love you back to life. My arms are wide open. You are safe with Me.

Week 2: Letting Go and Learning to Trust God's Love

Day 1: Facing the Pain of Letting Go

Scripture: Psalm 34:18

"The Lord is close to the brokenhearted and saves those who are crushed in spirit."

Instruction: Acknowledge the pain that comes with letting go of relationships or patterns that have hurt you. It's okay to feel broken. God is near.

Reflection: Journal about what feels hardest to release right now. What fears or doubts come up when you think about letting go?

Action: Pray and ask God to comfort your broken heart today. Write down any feelings or thoughts He brings to you.

Day 2: Understanding God's Perfect Love

Scripture: 1 John 4:18

"There is no fear in love. But perfect love drives out fear."

Instruction: Consider how God's love is different from what you've experienced before. His love is perfect and casts out fear.

Reflection: Write about what fear or insecurity you want God's love to conquer in your life.

Action: Repeat this truth aloud several times today: "God's perfect love drives out fear in me."

Day 3: Trusting God's Timing

Scripture: Ecclesiastes 3:1

"For everything there is a season, and a time for every matter under heaven."

Instruction: Trust that God's timing is perfect, even when waiting feels hard or uncertain.

Reflection: Journal about areas where you struggle with patience or control. How can you surrender those to God?

Action: Write a short prayer asking God for patience and trust in His timing.

Day 4: Replacing Old Lies with God's Truth

Scripture: Romans 12:2

"Do not be conformed to this world, but be transformed by the renewing of your mind."

Instruction: Identify lies you've believed about love, yourself, or your worth that need to be replaced with God's truth.

Reflection: Write down one lie and then write the corresponding truth from God's Word.

Action: Memorize the truth you wrote today and speak it aloud when negative thoughts come.

Day 5: Embracing Your Identity in Christ

Scripture: Ephesians 2:10

"For we are God's handiwork, created in Christ Jesus to do good works."

Instruction: Today, focus on who you are in Christ—valued, chosen, and beloved.

Reflection: Write a list of 3–5 qualities or promises God says about you.

Action: Stand in front of a mirror and declare those truths over yourself.

Day 6: Opening Your Heart to God's Love

Scripture: Psalm 36:7

"How priceless is your unfailing love, O God! People take refuge in the shadow of your wings."

Instruction: Invite God's love to heal the places your heart has guarded or closed off.

Reflection: Journal about what it would feel like to fully rest in God's love and protection.

Action: Spend 10 minutes today resting in God's presence. Imagine yourself safe under His wings.

Day 7: Moving Forward in Freedom

Scripture: 2 Corinthians 3:17

"Now the Lord is the Spirit, and where the Spirit of the Lord is, there is freedom."

Instruction: Celebrate the freedom you are stepping into by letting go and trusting God's love.

Reflection: Write a letter to God thanking Him for the freedom He's giving you.

Action: Make a plan to continue nurturing your relationship with God this week—through prayer, worship, or fellowship.

Week 2 Group Discussion Questions: Letting Go and Learning to Trust God's Love

1. Opening: What was a key takeaway or challenge from this week's devotional for you personally?
2. Letting go of toxic love or patterns is hard. What emotions surfaced for you when you reflected on what you need to release?
3. How have you experienced fear around love or relationships? How does 1 John 4:18 challenge those fears?
4. What does trusting God's timing look like in your life? How have you learned to be patient—or struggled with it?
5. We talked about replacing old lies with God's truth. What lies have been hardest for you to let go of? What truths from God's Word help you fight those lies?
6. How does embracing your identity in Christ—being God's handiwork—change how you see yourself and your relationships?
7. What practical steps can you take this week to open your heart more fully to God's love and protection?
8. How can this group encourage and hold each other accountable in trusting God's love more deeply?

Closing Prayer:

God, seal this week's work in my heart. When I'm tempted to pick back up what I laid down, remind me of Your faithfulness. Help me see Your love as trustworthy, steady, and true. I surrender again. Amen.

Healing Activity: "The Love Letter Exchange"

Instructions:

Write a raw, honest letter to God expressing your fears around letting go. Pour out your doubts, your hesitations, your pain. Then pause, pray, and write a letter from God to you—what you believe He would say in response.

Let His truth meet your vulnerability. Read both aloud to yourself and allow the exchange to minister to your soul.

Week 3: Breaking Soul Ties and Reclaiming Your Identity

Theme Recap:

T his week, you'll confront and break the soul ties that have kept you emotionally, spiritually, and even physically connected to people who no longer belong in your life. But more than just breaking ties—you're reclaiming who you are in Christ. You are not what happened to you. You are not who left or who failed to love you. You are God's beloved daughter, and this is your time to return to that truth.

Anchor Scripture:

"Do you not know that your bodies are temples of the Holy Spirit, who is in you… You are not your own; you were bought at a price. Therefore honor God with your bodies."
   – 1 Corinthians 6:19–20 (NIV)

Devotional Thought:

Soul ties are more than memories—they are emotional, spiritual, and sometimes sexual bonds that keep you attached to someone long after the relationship ends. But God has given you the authority to break every tie that is not rooted in Him. It's time to sever those connections and take back the pieces of your heart you gave away. You are not less because someone mishandled you. You are whole in Christ—and He's ready to walk you into a new identity that isn't shaped by past bonds, but by divine truth.

Reflection Questions:

1. Who or what are you still spiritually and emotionally tied to?
2. How have these soul ties affected the way you see yourself and your worth?
3. What do you believe God is saying about who you really are?

Journal Prompt:

Write the names of people you feel tied to emotionally or spiritually, even if you're no longer in contact. For each name, write a prayer of release and a declaration of who you are without that tie. Example: "I release [Name] in the name of Jesus. I am not bound to them. I am free, whole, and restored in my identity as God's daughter."

Prayer:

God, I break every ungodly soul tie in my life—ties created through trauma, sexual intimacy, emotional dependence, or false identity. I take back what I lost, and I surrender my heart to You. Heal me where I've been wounded. Restore me where I've been diminished. I declare that I am Yours, fully and forever. In Jesus' name, amen.

Action Step:

Take communion this week as an act of spiritual cleansing and covenant renewal with God. Declare aloud: "I am no longer tied to my past. I am tied to the blood of Jesus, and He is my new beginning."

God's Whisper:

Daughter, I've seen what tied you down and kept you small. But I'm cutting the cords of bondage. You are not forgotten. You are not defiled. You are Mine. Rise up and walk in the identity I gave you before the world ever touched you.

Week 3: Breaking Soul Ties and Reclaiming Your Identity

This week is about cutting ties with people and emotional connections that have kept you bound, ashamed, or confused. You'll begin to reclaim who you are—not who your past says you are, but who God declares you to be. It's time to walk in freedom.

Day 1: What Is a Soul Tie?

Scripture: Proverbs 4:23
   "Above all else, guard your heart, for everything you do flows from it."
   Instruction: Today, explore what a soul tie is—a deep emotional or spiritual connection that can keep you tied to someone long after the relationship has ended.
   Reflection: Write about a connection from your past that still affects you. What emotions or memories are hard to shake?
   Action: Ask God to reveal any unhealthy soul ties you need to release. Write them down honestly.

Day 2: When Love Becomes a Chain

Scripture: Galatians 5:1
   "It is for freedom that Christ has set us free…"
   Instruction: Even if it felt like love, not all love is freeing. Reflect on how unhealthy emotional attachments can feel like chains rather than love.

Reflection: Think of a time you knew something was wrong but stayed because of the emotional pull. Journal how that affected your sense of self.

Action: Declare today out loud: "God wants me free." Speak it in faith even if you don't feel it yet.

Day 3: Renouncing the Ties That Bind

Scripture: 2 Corinthians 10:4-5

"…we demolish arguments and every pretension… and we take captive every thought to make it obedient to Christ."

Instruction: Breaking a soul tie involves renouncing the emotional, spiritual, and even physical ties that bound you.

Reflection: Write a letter of release. Name the tie. Renounce it in prayer. Release that person and reclaim your identity.

Action: Tear up or burn the letter as a symbol of your freedom (safely). Say aloud: "I am no longer tied to this pain."

Day 4: Who Does God Say I Am?

Scripture: Isaiah 43:1

"Do not fear, for I have redeemed you; I have called you by name; you are Mine."

Instruction: After letting go, there is often a feeling of emptiness. Fill that space with God's truth about who you are.

Reflection: List 3–5 things God says about you in His Word. Reflect on how believing these truths can help you heal.

Action: Post your list somewhere visible. Speak them over yourself each day this week.

Day 5: Forgiving Yourself and Reclaiming Your Worth

Scripture: Romans 8:1
"Therefore, there is now no condemnation for those who are in Christ Jesus."

Instruction: Breaking soul ties also means forgiving yourself for what you allowed, ignored, or endured.

Reflection: Write a prayer of forgiveness—not to anyone else, but to yourself. Let go of shame.

Action: Look in the mirror and say: "I forgive you. You didn't know your worth then, but you're learning now."

Day 6: Receiving God's Healing Love

Scripture: Psalm 147:3
"He heals the brokenhearted and binds up their wounds."

Instruction: Let yourself be loved. After all the inner work, allow God to simply love you back to life.

Reflection: How have you seen God's love healing parts of you already? What still needs healing?

Action: Spend quiet time with worship music. Let God minister to the places that still feel fragile.

Day 7: Walking in Freedom

Scripture: John 8:36
"So if the Son sets you free, you will be free indeed."

Instruction: You are not who you were when you started this journey. You are walking in newness and freedom.

Reflection: Write a declaration of freedom. Speak over your life what you believe God is doing in you.

Action: Celebrate in some way—light a candle, journal a praise report, or take a prayer walk. Mark your freedom.

Week 3 Group Discussion Questions

1. Opening: What moment or day this week impacted you the most emotionally or spiritually?
2. How would you define a soul tie in your own words, and why is it important to break them?
3. What past relationship or attachment was hardest for you to let go of, and why?
4. Did you find it difficult to forgive yourself for past choices? What helped you move forward?
5. Which scripture or truth this week spoke loudest to your heart?
6. How has your view of your identity in Christ changed through this week's devotionals?
7. What's one way the group can pray for you this week as you walk out your healing and freedom?

Soul Tie Breaker Prayer

Heavenly Father,

I come before You with a heart that desires freedom. You know every hidden place within me—every soul tie, every emotional bond, every unholy connection I've carried, knowingly or unknowingly.

Right now, in the mighty name of Jesus, I break every soul tie that has kept me bound. I sever every unhealthy emotional, spiritual, and physical connection that does not honor You. I release the people, memories, and emotional attachments that have held me captive. I renounce the lies I believed—that I was unworthy of love, that I had to settle for less, that my identity was tied to a relationship instead of to You.

I receive Your forgiveness, Lord. I forgive myself. I am no longer defined by my past choices, but by Your grace. Wash me clean. Heal every broken place. Fill every empty space. Restore what was stolen from me—my peace, my joy, my identity, my worth.

Father, I declare that I am Yours. Fully, freely, and forever. Thank You for calling me by name and making me whole again. In Jesus' name, Amen.

Affirmation Cards: Reclaiming My Identity in Christ

Card 1:

I am no longer tied to my past.

I am walking in the freedom of Christ.

(John 8:36)

Card 2:

God has called me by name—I am His.

I am chosen, not forsaken.

(Isaiah 43:1)

Card 3:

I forgive myself for what I didn't know, and I embrace who I am becoming in God.

(Romans 8:1)

Card 4:

My value is not in who left, but in the One who stays.

(Deuteronomy 31:6)

Card 5:

God's love is healing me—mind, body, and soul.

(Psalm 147:3)

Card 6:

I do not need to go back.

Freedom is ahead of me.

God is with me.

(Galatians 5:1)

Closing Prayer:

Jesus, thank You for breaking every chain and severing every soul tie that was not sent by You. I receive Your healing and step boldly into who I am—whole, free, and fiercely loved. Amen.

Healing Activity: "The Soul Tie Cutting Ritual"

Instructions:

On individual slips of paper, write the names of people or past versions of yourself that you feel tied to. One by one, say aloud: "I cut this soul tie in the name of Jesus and reclaim my wholeness." Then tear or safely burn each slip of paper. Follow this with a moment of prayer and stillness. End by saying: "I am free."

Week 4: Healing the Wounds of Rejection

Theme Recap:

This week, we're going to the root—where the wound first began. Rejection often enters our lives through childhood, failed relationships, or unmet expectations. It leaves us questioning our worth, our place, and even God's love. But the truth is: you were never a mistake. And rejection is not your identity—it's a wound that Jesus came to heal. God is ready to fill the spaces where others walked away.

Anchor Scripture:

"Though my father and mother forsake me, the Lord will receive me."
  – Psalm 27:10 (NIV)

Devotional Thought:

Rejection feels like being unseen, unwanted, and unworthy. It can follow you into friendships, love, church—even your self-image. But God specializes in the rejected. Jesus Himself was "despised and rejected by men," yet He became the cornerstone. That means your story doesn't end in abandonment—it begins again in acceptance. God sees you, receives you, and calls you chosen. You don't have to live trying to earn love. His love is already yours.

Reflection Questions:

1. What is your earliest memory of feeling rejected?
2. How has rejection shaped the way you view yourself and others?
3. What would healing look like in that place of rejection?

Journal Prompt:

Write a letter to the version of yourself who first felt rejected—whether a little girl, a teenager, or a woman in a broken relationship. Speak life, truth, and love over her. Let God's voice speak through your pen.

Prayer:

Lord, I bring You the pieces of my heart that have been broken by rejection. I've carried this wound for far too long. I've allowed it to define me, silence me, and steal my joy. But no more. I give You the pain. Heal me in the places no one else can reach. Show me what it means to be chosen, accepted, and completely loved by You. In Jesus' name, amen.

Action Step:

Each day this week, speak this declaration aloud: "I am not rejected. I am accepted, embraced, and deeply loved by God." Write it on a sticky note. Post it where you'll see it often.

God's Whisper:

My daughter, I know the ache of being left behind. But I will never leave you. You are My beloved. I picked you, pursued you, and made room for you at My table. Don't look back—look at Me. I'm the Father who never turns away.

Week 4: Healing the Wounds of Rejection

You've broken ties, faced truth, and embraced freedom. But rejection still leaves a deep bruise—one that whispers, you're not enough. This week, God wants to uproot those lies and show you the steady, healing power of His love. He didn't reject you—He chose you.

Day 1: Recognizing the Root of Rejection

Scripture: Psalm 27:10

"Though my father and mother forsake me, the Lord will receive me."

Instruction: Trace the root. Rejection doesn't start in a relationship—it often begins in childhood, family wounds, or early betrayal.

Reflection: Where did rejection first take root in your life? How has it shaped your decisions or relationships?

Action: Write a letter to God about that pain. Be honest—He can handle your hurt.

Day 2: Rejection Is Not Your Identity

Scripture: Ephesians 1:4–5

"He chose us in Him before the foundation of the world…"

Instruction: You are not what someone else didn't choose. God's choice cancels man's rejection.

Reflection: What labels have you carried because of rejection? How does God's Word contradict those labels?

Action: List those false labels. Cross them out. Then write the truth: Chosen. Loved. Accepted.

Day 3: When Love Feels Conditional

Scripture: Romans 5:8

"But God demonstrates His own love for us in this: While we were still sinners, Christ died for us."

Instruction: Many of us have learned to perform for love. But God's love is unconditional.

Reflection: Have you ever felt like you had to earn someone's love? What did that do to your self-worth?

Action: Sit with this truth: You are loved without having to perform. Say it out loud. Write it where you'll see it often.

Day 4: Uprooting the Lie "I'm Not Enough"

Scripture: 2 Corinthians 12:9

"My grace is sufficient for you, for My power is made perfect in weakness."

Instruction: Rejection often plants the lie that you're not enough. But God says His grace covers every gap.

Reflection: Where do you feel "not enough"? How can God's grace meet you in that place?

Action: Pray: Lord, I give You every place in me that feels unworthy. Remind me of who I am in You.

Day 5: Reclaiming Your Confidence

Scripture: Hebrews 10:35

"So do not throw away your confidence; it will be richly rewarded."

Instruction: Rejection steals confidence. But your confidence is not in you—it's in Christ.

Reflection: What would it look like to walk confidently in your identity? What would you stop hiding from?

Action: Write an "I am" statement rooted in faith. Example: I am bold, because Christ goes before me.

Day 6: Love That Never Walks Away

Scripture: Deuteronomy 31:8
"The Lord Himself goes before you and will be with you; He will never leave you nor forsake you."

Instruction: God's love is consistent. He doesn't ghost, abandon, or betray. He stays.

Reflection: How have human relationships distorted your view of God's love? What would it feel like to fully trust Him?

Action: Rest. Spend quiet time soaking in worship or silence. Let yourself be loved.

Day 7: You Are the One He Loves

Scripture: Zephaniah 3:17
"He will take great delight in you… He will rejoice over you with singing."

Instruction: You are the one God rejoices over—not barely tolerates. You are deeply wanted.

Reflection: How does knowing God delights in you change your view of yourself?

Action: Write a love letter from God to your heart. Let the Holy Spirit guide your words. Then read it aloud.

Week 4 Group Discussion Questions

1. What rejection wound surfaced for you this week? How did you handle it emotionally and spiritually?
2. Which day's devotional felt the most healing or personal? Why?
3. Have you struggled with believing you had to earn love? What has that looked like in your life?
4. What false identity have you carried due to rejection—and what truth from God replaced it?

5. What did your "I am" faith statement say? How did it feel to declare it?
6. How can this group be a safe place for you to rebuild confidence and trust?
7. What would trusting God's love daily look like for you in this season?

Closing Prayer:

Jesus, I lay down the lies that rejection has spoken over me. I choose to believe what You say: that I am fearfully and wonderfully made, that I belong, and that You are enough. Heal my heart and rewrite my story with Your love. Amen.

Healing Activity: "Release & Receive" Mirror Exercise

Instructions:

Stand in front of a mirror. Look yourself in the eyes and say:

"I release the pain of rejection. I release the belief that I am not enough. I receive the truth that I am loved by God—fully and forever."

Repeat this daily. Journal how your self-image begins to shift.

Week 5: Waiting Well – Trusting God's Timing

Theme Recap:

This week invites you into the sacred space of waiting—where God often does His deepest work. Waiting isn't punishment; it's preparation. And while it may feel like delay, it's actually divine timing unfolding. When we learn to wait well, we stop striving, comparing, and doubting. We start trusting, resting, and expecting. God is never late. He's building something beautiful—and that includes you.

Anchor Scripture:

"But they that wait upon the Lord shall renew their strength; they shall mount up with wings as eagles; they shall run, and not be weary; and they shall walk, and not faint."
   – Isaiah 40:31 (KJV)

Devotional Thought:

Waiting doesn't mean God has forgotten you—it means He's forming you. In the silence, He is strengthening your faith. In the pause, He's developing your character. The enemy wants you to believe that if it hasn't happened yet, it won't. But God's promises are not dead; they're being matured. When you trust His timing, you release control and make room for miracles. Waiting well isn't passive—it's powerful.

Reflection Questions:

1. What are you waiting on God for right now?
2. How have you struggled with impatience, comparison, or doubt during the wait?
3. What would it look like to trust God fully with your timeline?

Journal Prompt:

Write a letter to God about the thing you've been waiting for the longest. Be honest. Then write a response as if God is speaking back to you—reassuring you of His timing and faithfulness.

Prayer:

Lord, waiting isn't easy. Sometimes it hurts. Sometimes it feels like You're silent. But I choose to trust You, even when I don't understand. Strengthen me in the wait. Teach me to worship instead of worry, to rest instead of rush. I believe that what You have for me is worth every moment of preparation. In Jesus' name, amen.

Action Step:

Create a "Trust Timeline." On one side, list promises you've seen God fulfill in the past. On the other, write what you're currently waiting on. Let your past victories remind you that God has always been on time—and He still is.

God's Whisper:

Daughter, I'm not withholding—I'm preparing. What you call delay, I call design. I know the weight of your prayers. I see the longing in your heart. But I need you to trust that I'm weaving something far greater than you imagined. Wait on Me. I'm worth it.

Week 5: Waiting Well — Trusting God's Timing

Waiting can feel like torture when your heart still longs for love, healing, or restoration. But this week, we shift our perspective: waiting is not a delay in your destiny—it's God's protection and preparation for the right thing at the right time.

Day 1: Why Am I Still Waiting?

Scripture: Isaiah 40:31
   "But those who wait on the Lord shall renew their strength…"
   Instruction: The delay doesn't mean denial. God is doing a deeper work within you.
   Reflection: Are you tired of waiting? What has waiting brought out of you—faith or frustration?
   Action: Write a prayer of surrender. Acknowledge your weariness and invite God into your waiting season.

Day 2: Trusting What You Can't See

Scripture: Hebrews 11:1
   "Now faith is confidence in what we hope for and assurance about what we do not see."
   Instruction: Waiting well means walking by faith, not by sight.
   Reflection: Where are you tempted to take matters into your own hands?

What would trusting God look like instead?

Action: Draw a line down your journal. On one side, write what you're afraid of. On the other, write what God promises.

Day 3: The Beauty of Becoming

Scripture: Ecclesiastes 3:11

"He has made everything beautiful in its time…"

Instruction: You're not just waiting for something—you're becoming someone.

Reflection: What part of your character is God refining in this season?

Action: Make a list of personal growth you've seen in yourself since choosing to follow God's path.

Day 4: When Waiting Feels Lonely

Scripture: Psalm 25:3

"No one who hopes in you will ever be put to shame…"

Instruction: Waiting can feel like being forgotten. But God never forgets His daughters.

Reflection: What lie has loneliness made you believe about God or yourself?

Action: Replace it with truth. Declare: I am not forgotten. I am loved, seen, and held by God.

Day 5: Protecting Your Peace While You Wait

Scripture: Philippians 4:6–7

"Do not be anxious about anything… and the peace of God… will guard your hearts and minds…"

Instruction: Peace isn't the absence of waiting—it's the presence of God in the wait.

Reflection: What steals your peace most when you're waiting?

Action: Write a "peace plan": ways you'll stay grounded in God during moments of doubt or discouragement.

Day 6: Choosing Purpose Over Panic

Scripture: Romans 8:28
"And we know that in all things God works for the good…"
Instruction: Don't just wait passively—wait purposefully. God wants to use this time to grow your calling.
Reflection: What can you pour your energy into while you wait? Where is God nudging you to serve, grow, or create?
Action: Commit to doing one thing this week that aligns with your purpose.

Day 7: The Reward of the Wait

Scripture: Galatians 6:9
"Let us not become weary in doing good, for at the proper time we will reap a harvest…"
Instruction: Your waiting will not be wasted. God sees, honors, and rewards your faithfulness.
Reflection: How has God already met you in the waiting? What blessings have come through the process?
Action: Celebrate! Write a gratitude list of things you now see clearly because you waited.

Week 5 Group Discussion Questions

1. What area of your life feels hardest to wait in right now?
2. How do you usually react to waiting? Have you seen growth in how you wait?
3. Which day this week helped shift your mindset the most—and why?
4. What has God been teaching you about His timing?

5. How have you seen purpose in your waiting?

6. What lies do you battle while waiting—and what truth are you holding onto instead?

7. What's one thing you want to do differently as you continue waiting for God's best?

Closing Prayer:

God, thank You for being patient with me as I learn to trust Your timing. Help me release the pressure to make things happen on my own. Teach me to find joy, purpose, and peace in the wait. I believe that You are faithful to finish what You've started in me. Amen.

Healing Activity: "The Waiting Jar"

Instructions:

Find a small jar or box. On slips of paper, write the things you're currently waiting on God to do—dreams, prayers, breakthroughs. Each time you feel anxious or impatient, go to the jar. Hold one request and say: "God, I trust You with this." Over time, watch how faith replaces fear.

Week 6: Falling in Love with God

Theme Recap:

This week, we shift our focus from waiting on God to being with Him. It's time to fall in love—not with an idea, not with a blessing, but with God Himself. He is not distant. He's not withholding. He is near, pursuing, gentle, and deeply invested in your heart. God wants more than your obedience—He desires intimacy. This week is about learning to love Him back with your whole heart.

Anchor Scripture:

"Love the Lord your God with all your heart and with all your soul and with all your mind and with all your strength."
  – Mark 12:30 (NIV)

Devotional Thought:

Falling in love with God is not a one-time event—it's a daily choice. The more time you spend with Him, the more you'll see His heart and feel His love. He's not like anyone else who hurt you, left you, or made you prove your worth. He's safe. He's faithful. And He wants to be your first love. This kind of love heals you, fulfills you, and changes how you see everything—including yourself.

Reflection Questions:

1. What has kept you from fully opening your heart to God?
2. What does being "in love with God" look like in your everyday life?
3. How would your relationship with God change if you believed He delighted in you?

Journal Prompt:

Describe a moment when you felt closest to God. What made that moment so special? How can you create more space for that closeness in your daily life?

Prayer:

Father, I want to love You not just with my words, but with my heart. Teach me how to fall in love with You again. Strip away distractions, fears, and anything that stands between us. Make me sensitive to Your presence. Let our relationship be my most treasured connection. In Jesus' name, amen.

Action Step:

Plan a "date" with God this week—just the two of you. Take a walk, journal in a quiet place, or worship without distraction. Let it be intentional. No requests. No lists. Just love and presence.

God's Whisper:

Beloved, I have always been the One pursuing you. In every heartbreak, I stayed. In every silent moment, I listened. You were made for My love, and My love was made to fill you. Let Me be the One your soul longs for. I'm here. I always have been.

Week 6: Falling in Love with God

You've let go. You've healed. You've waited. Now, it's time to receive the greatest love you'll ever know—the love of your Heavenly Father. His love is not like man's love. It doesn't leave. It doesn't lie. It transforms you from the inside out.

Day 1: God Desires You

Scripture: James 4:8
   "Draw near to God, and He will draw near to you."
   Instruction: God isn't distant. He longs to be close to you, to know you and be known by you.
   Reflection: Do you believe God desires a deep, intimate relationship with you?
   Action: Start your day by saying, "God, I want to know You more. Teach me how to love You deeply."

Day 2: A Love That Sees the Real You

Scripture: Psalm 139:1–2
   "You have searched me, Lord, and you know me…"
   Instruction: God sees every part of you and still chooses to love you fully.
   Reflection: What parts of yourself have you tried to hide—even from God?
   Action: Journal: If God sees and loves me anyway, I no longer need to hide…

Day 3: Worship—The Language of Intimacy

Scripture: John 4:23
   "True worshipers will worship the Father in spirit and truth…"
   Instruction: Worship is how we pour our love on God. It softens our hearts and deepens our connection with Him.

Reflection: What does your worship life look like? Is it a duty—or a love offering?

Action: Spend intentional time today in worship—music, silence, prayer, dance—whatever draws you near to Him.

Day 4: God Is a Jealous Lover

Scripture: Exodus 34:14

"Do not worship any other god, for the Lord… is a jealous God."

Instruction: God wants your whole heart. Not just what's left after chasing other loves.

Reflection: Is there anything still competing with God for your affection?

Action: List distractions or idols. Ask God to help you surrender them one by one.

Day 5: Letting God Romance Your Heart

Scripture: Hosea 2:14

"I will allure her and bring her into the wilderness and speak tenderly to her…"

Instruction: God's love is gentle, persistent, and healing. He knows how to pursue your heart in a way no one else can.

Reflection: When was the last time you felt pursued by God?

Action: Take yourself on a "date" with God today. Go for a walk, drink tea, write a letter to Him—whatever reminds you that you are deeply loved.

Day 6: Loving God With Your Whole Heart

Scripture: Matthew 22:37

"Love the Lord your God with all your heart and with all your soul and with all your mind."

Instruction: God wants more than pieces of your love—He wants your whole heart.

Reflection: What would it look like to love God with your whole self—not just when you feel emotional, but with intention?

Action: Write a love letter to God. Pour out your gratitude, affection, and commitment.

Day 7: His Love Will Never Let You Go

Scripture: Romans 8:38–39

"Nothing can separate us from the love of God that is in Christ Jesus..."

Instruction: His love is eternal. No failure, heartbreak, or fear can separate you from Him.

Reflection: What fear or lie tries to convince you that God will stop loving you?

Action: Affirm daily: "God's love for me is unshakable, unstoppable, and eternal."

Week 6 Group Discussion Questions

1. What does "falling in love with God" mean to you personally?
2. Which day this week made you feel most connected to God?
3. What did you discover about the way God desires you?
4. Are there still places in your heart you find difficult to give to God? Why?
5. How has worship shifted your relationship with God?
6. What idols or distractions are you surrendering so God can have your whole heart?
7. What practical steps will you take to continue nurturing your intimacy with God after this study?

Closing Prayer:

God, thank You for not giving up on me—even when I gave You only pieces of my heart. Today I choose You. Not for what You can give me, but for who You are. Teach me how to be in love with You. Make You the center of my life, my peace, and my joy. Amen.

Healing Activity: "Love Letter Exchange"

Instructions:

Write a love letter to God. Express your gratitude, admiration, and desire for deeper connection. Then sit in silence and write a letter from God to you—allow His Spirit to speak words of affection, acceptance, and intimacy over your life. Keep both letters in a safe place and return to them when you feel distant from Him.

Week 7: Walking in Purpose and Identity

Theme Recap:

This week is all about becoming who you were born to be. You were never meant to live beneath your calling, in fear or confusion. God has written purpose into your DNA, and identity into your spirit. The more you align with His truth, the more confident, powerful, and free you'll become. You don't have to keep searching—your identity is in Christ, and your purpose flows from that truth.

Anchor Scripture:

"For we are God's masterpiece. He has created us anew in Christ Jesus, so we can do the good things He planned for us long ago."
  – Ephesians 2:10 (NLT)

Devotional Thought:

You were not a mistake, and your life is not random. God didn't just save you—He called you. He didn't just forgive you—He anointed you. Every painful moment, every trial you've survived, is now part of the story He will use for His glory. Your purpose is not something you have to figure out on your own. It's revealed as you walk in obedience, identity, and love. When you truly believe who you are, you'll begin to do what you were created for.

Reflection Questions:

1. What lies have you believed about who you are or what you're capable of?
2. When do you feel most aligned with your purpose?
3. What has God revealed to you this season about your gifts, calling, or spiritual identity?

Journal Prompt:

Write a declaration about who you are in Christ. Start with "I am…" and list everything you believe God says about you—boldly and without apology.

Prayer:

God, thank You for creating me on purpose, with purpose. Forgive me for shrinking back, doubting, or comparing myself to others. Today I receive my true identity in You. Teach me how to walk boldly in the calling You've placed on my life. I surrender my plans for Your divine purpose. In Jesus' name, amen.

Action Step:

Make a list of your spiritual gifts, natural talents, and passions. Pray over them, and ask God how He wants to use them. Take one step this week—big or small—toward walking boldly in one of those areas.

God's Whisper:

Daughter, I placed greatness in you. You are not forgotten, overlooked, or without direction. You were born for such a time as this. Stop running from who you are. Step into it. The world is waiting for the light I've placed inside of you.

Week 7: Walking in Purpose and Identity

You are no longer who you were when you began this journey. You've let go of toxic love, healed from soul ties, sat in the wilderness with God, and found the courage to love Him deeply. Now, it's time to rise up and walk in everything He created you to be.

Day 1: You Are Who God Says You Are

Scripture: 1 Peter 2:9

"You are a chosen people, a royal priesthood, a holy nation, God's special possession…"

Instruction: Your identity isn't in your pain, your past, or your mistakes. It's in Christ.

Reflection: Whose voice has defined you the most—God's, or someone else's?

Action: Write out an "I am" identity list based solely on what the Word says about you.

Day 2: From Wounded to Warrior

Scripture: Joel 2:25

"I will restore to you the years the locusts have eaten…"

Instruction: God restores—and then He sends. You are not only healed; you are equipped.

Reflection: How have your wounds equipped you to help others?

Action: Write a short testimony of how God has transformed part of your story.

Day 3: You Have a Calling

Scripture: Ephesians 2:10

"For we are God's workmanship… created to do good works, which God prepared in advance for us to do."

Instruction: You were made for purpose. You were created to do something only you can do.

Reflection: What passion or burden has God placed on your heart during this healing journey?

Action: Journal one small, bold step you can take toward living in your God-given purpose.

Day 4: No More Shrinking Back

Scripture: Hebrews 10:39

"But we are not those who shrink back and are destroyed, but of those who believe and are saved."

Instruction: Fear no longer has the final say in your life. Boldness is your new posture.

Reflection: Where are you still playing small—and why?

Action: Write a declaration that begins with: "I will no longer shrink back from…"

Day 5: Becoming a Light for Others

Scripture: Matthew 5:14

"You are the light of the world…"

Instruction: Your healing is not just for you. It's for those who need the light you now carry.

Reflection: Who in your life needs the light and healing you've experienced?

Action: Write down the name of someone you can encourage, pray for, or share your journey with this week.

Day 6: Living Authentically and Free

Scripture: Galatians 5:1

"It is for freedom that Christ has set us free…"

Instruction: You don't have to pretend, perform, or prove anymore. You are free to be fully you.

Reflection: What does freedom look like for you now?

Action: List what you're no longer tolerating in your life now that you're walking in freedom.

Day 7: Commissioned to Rise

Scripture: Isaiah 60:1

"Arise, shine, for your light has come, and the glory of the Lord rises upon you."

Instruction: You've healed. You've grown. Now, it's time to rise up and walk in everything God destined you to be.

Reflection: How has this journey changed you?

Action: Stand in the mirror and say out loud: "I am healed, whole, chosen, and called. I rise in purpose and power."

Week 7 Group Discussion Questions

1. How do you now see yourself differently than when this study began?
2. What part of your story do you believe God wants to use for His glory?
3. Where are you feeling led to serve, speak, write, teach, or give?
4. What lies are you laying down to walk confidently in your new identity?
5. What steps will you take to walk in your purpose with boldness?
6. How can this group encourage one another to rise and remain accountable?
7. In what way do you feel you are now becoming the woman God designed you to be?

Closing Prayer:

Father, I give You my identity and my future. Shape me. Use me. Show me how to walk like Your daughter—fearless, confident, and full of purpose. Let my life reflect Your glory. Amen.

Healing Activity: "Purpose Vision Board"

Instructions:

Gather words, pictures, scriptures, and symbols that represent your God-given purpose and identity. Create a physical or digital vision board. As you place each item, pray: "Lord, align my life with Your will and purpose." Post it where you can see it often to keep you grounded and inspired.

Week 8: Becoming the Woman God Designed

Theme Recap:

This final week is about becoming—fully, freely, and fearlessly—the woman God designed you to be. Everything you've released, healed, surrendered, and discovered has brought you to this moment. You are not just surviving anymore—you are stepping into wholeness. This is your season to rise, walk boldly in identity, and live from a place of divine fulfillment. You are becoming everything He had in mind when He formed you.

Anchor Scripture:

"She is clothed with strength and dignity; she can laugh at the days to come."
 – Proverbs 31:25 (NIV)

Devotional Thought:

Becoming is a process, but it's also a decision. You don't need to strive to be enough—you already are. God didn't make a mistake when He made you. You are fearfully and wonderfully made, deeply loved, and fully equipped to walk in destiny. When you let go of the past, embrace His truth, and allow healing to transform you, you become the woman you were always meant to be. That woman is bold, radiant, healed, and whole.

Reflection Questions:

1. In what ways have you grown over the past 8 weeks?
2. What part of your identity are you now ready to fully own and walk in?
3. What does it look like to live as the healed, empowered woman God designed?

Journal Prompt:

Write a letter to your future self. Encourage her, remind her who she is, and declare the kind of woman she will continue to become through God's strength and love.

Prayer:

Father, thank You for walking with me through this journey. I release every version of me that wasn't healed, whole, or free. Today, I step into the woman You've called me to be—confident, loved, and purposed. Continue to shape me, use me, and lead me into the life You designed just for me. In Jesus' name, amen.

Action Step:

Write a personal mission statement. Include your identity in Christ, your God-given purpose, and the legacy you want to leave behind. Let it be your compass moving forward.

God's Whisper:

Daughter, look at you—you're rising. You've been broken, but now you're whole. You've cried, but now you laugh. You once doubted, but now you believe. You are everything I designed you to be: chosen, anointed, fearless, and free. Stay close to Me. The best is still ahead.

Week 8: Becoming the Woman God Designed

This is your final week. You've walked through the wilderness, released soul ties, faced deep rejection, waited in surrender, and discovered the joy of falling in love with God. Now it's time to live as the healed, whole, bold woman God designed. This is not the end of your journey—it's the beginning of your new life.

Day 1: God's Masterpiece

Scripture: Ephesians 2:10
   "For we are God's masterpiece. He has created us anew in Christ Jesus…"
   Instruction: You are not a mistake. You are a masterpiece—intentionally created by God with purpose, power, and beauty.
   Reflection: What parts of yourself do you now see through God's eyes?
   Action: Write a thank-you letter to God for the woman He's shaping you into.

Day 2: Stepping Boldly Into Your New Identity

Scripture: 2 Corinthians 5:17
   "If anyone is in Christ, she is a new creation…"
   Instruction: You're not who you used to be. You don't have to carry the past with you into this new season.
   Reflection: What mindsets or habits must stay in the past as you move

forward?

Action: Symbolically write down what you're leaving behind—and tear it up or burn it as an act of release.

Day 3: A Life That Reflects His Glory

Scripture: 1 Corinthians 10:31

"So whether you eat or drink or whatever you do, do it all for the glory of God."

Instruction: Every part of your life is now a reflection of God's healing power and redeeming love.

Reflection: What does it look like for your relationships, words, and choices to reflect God?

Action: Choose one area of your life to intentionally surrender to His glory today.

Day 4: Walking in Authority

Scripture: Luke 10:19

"I have given you authority… to overcome all the power of the enemy…"

Instruction: You are not powerless. You have spiritual authority through Christ to say no to fear, shame, and anything that tries to pull you back.

Reflection: Where do you need to start walking in more spiritual authority?

Action: Declare aloud: "I walk in the authority of Christ. I will not return to bondage."

Day 5: Becoming a Vessel of Healing for Others

Scripture: 2 Corinthians 1:4

"He comforts us… so that we can comfort others…"

Instruction: Your story is now a tool in God's hands. You're not just a survivor—you're a healer in the making.

Reflection: Who has God placed in your path that you can walk with through their healing journey?

Action: Write out a short "word of hope" you could speak to someone who feels stuck where you once were.

Day 6: Celebration Day — Honor Your Journey

Scripture: Nehemiah 8:10

"...The joy of the Lord is your strength."

Instruction: Take time to celebrate how far you've come. This healing was hard-fought. It deserves to be honored.

Reflection: What do you feel most proud of yourself for?

Action: Do something today to celebrate your spiritual growth—journaling, dancing, worshiping, even treating yourself.

Day 7: Commissioned to Rise

Scripture: Isaiah 61:3

"...They will be called oaks of righteousness, a planting of the Lord for the display of His splendor."

Instruction: This is your commissioning. You are not just healed—you are planted, strengthened, and sent.

Reflection: What is God calling you to rise into now?

Action: Stand, place your hand over your heart, and speak:

"I am healed. I am whole. I am chosen. I am called. I am a vessel of God's glory. I will walk boldly in my identity and purpose, in Jesus' name."

Week 8 Group Discussion Questions

1. In what ways have you changed since beginning this journey?
2. What parts of your healing were the hardest—but most powerful?
3. How do you now see yourself as a vessel for others' healing?
4. What does being "commissioned to rise" look like in your everyday life?

5. What spiritual disciplines will help you maintain the freedom you've gained?
6. How can this group support one another beyond the study?

Closing Prayer:

God, I don't want to go back. I am not who I was—I am who You've called me to be. Thank You for every step of this healing journey. Keep transforming me, leading me, and loving me. I am Yours. Fully. Finally. Forever. Amen.

Healing Activity: "Becoming Ceremony"

Instructions:

Write a "Becoming Declaration" that starts with: "Today, I declare that I am becoming…" Include every truth God has shown you about your identity, strength, healing, and purpose. Read it aloud. Light a candle, anoint your head or hands with oil, and thank God for the transformation He has started—and will continue—in your life.

Closing Group Activity: "The Becoming Circle"

Purpose:

To celebrate the transformation that has taken place, affirm one another, and declare God's truth as a community of healed and becoming women.

Instructions:

- Create a Safe, Sacred Space
- Set up the space with soft music, candles, or flowers—whatever makes it feel like a holy celebration. Provide each woman with a mirror, anointing oil, and a "Becoming Declaration" card.

Mirror Affirmations -Each woman looks into the mirror and declares who she is becoming in Christ. She speaks aloud a short affirmation like:

- "I am chosen. I am whole. I am who God says I am."

Anointing & Blessing-In pairs or small groups, women anoint each other's foreheads or hands with oil while speaking a blessing such as:

- "You are called. You are healed. Walk boldly in purpose."

Encouragement Circle-Go around the room and allow each woman to share one thing she's leaving behind and one thing she's stepping into. Encourage the group to respond with one unified declaration like:

- "Walk in freedom!" or "You were made for this!"

Read Aloud God's Whisper (from Week 8)

- Read it as a group or have a leader read it over the women.

A Personal Letter from the Author

Dear Beautiful Sister,

As we come to the end of this sacred journey, my heart is full. Writing this study guide wasn't just a task—it was a calling. And walking beside you these past eight weeks has been one of the greatest honors of my life.

I know that you didn't come to these pages by accident. Whether you arrived here broken, searching, weary, or simply hungry for something deeper, I want you to know this: God saw you coming. He's been preparing a table for your healing long before you even knew what you were thirsty for.

I have wept as I wrote. I have prayed over every word. Because I know what it is to long for healing, to ache for love, to be tired of empty promises and toxic cycles. And I also know what it is to finally say yes to God's love—and never look back.

You've done something courageous. You've confronted pain. You've uprooted lies. You've dared to believe that there is more. And you've taken steps toward freedom, wholeness, and divine purpose. That is no small thing. That is victory.

As you close this book, I pray it's not the end—but a beginning. I pray that your heart remains open, your spirit stays sensitive to His voice, and your feet stay grounded in truth. I pray you continue to fall in love with the God who already adores you. And I look forward—truly—to hearing the success stories that are being birthed through your testimony.

You are the woman God designed. And the world needs the healed, bold, purpose-filled version of you. So keep walking. Keep becoming. Keep

drinking deeply from the well that never runs dry.
  With love, pride, and great expectation for your future

Chanita R. Ramsey

Final Prayer of Commissioning

Heavenly Father,

Thank You for every woman gathered here today. You have carried her through dark places, through pain, through healing, and now into purpose. You have written her story with grace and strength. Today, we declare that she is no longer bound by fear, shame, or soul ties. She is healed. She is whole. She is free.

God, we commission her to walk boldly in the purpose You've placed within her. Let her rise with confidence, serve with compassion, and love with power. May she never forget who she is and Whose she is. Anoint her steps. Protect her journey. Multiply her impact. And may her life be a living testimony of Your faithfulness.

We bless her in the name of the Father, the Son, and the Holy Spirit. Amen.

Final Benediction

May the One who met you in the valley lift you to the mountain. May the tears you cried in the quiet become the rivers that nourish your next season.

May every lie that once chained you fall powerless at your feet.

And may truth rise within you like the morning sun—gentle, certain, and full of promise.

May you walk with the confidence of a woman who knows she is chosen.

May you love with the heart of one who has been healed by Love Himself.

May your past never speak louder than your purpose.

And may your soul always thirst—not for the things that fade—but for the One who satisfies.

As you go forward, may peace wrap around you like a shawl,

May joy bubble up from places that once held sorrow,

And may grace follow you, all the days of your life.

Daughter of the Most High,

You are becoming all God created you to be.

Drink deeply. Live boldly.

And never forget—you are so deeply loved.

Amen.